FAVORITE POEMS OF CHILDHOOD

FAVORITE POEMS
OF CHILDHOOD

ILLUSTRATED BY WALTER CRANE

GREEN TIGER PRESS
Published by Simon & Schuster
New York · London · Toronto · Sydney · Tokyo · Singapore

GREEN TIGER PRESS
Simon & Schuster Building
Rockefeller Center
1230 Avenue of the Americas
New York, New York 10020
Volume copyright © 1993 by The Albion Press Ltd
All rights reserved including the right of reproduction
in whole or in part in any form.
GREEN TIGER PRESS is an imprint of Simon & Schuster.
Conceived, designed and produced by
The Albion Press Ltd, England
Manufactured in Singapore by Tien Wah Press
10 9 8 7 6 5 4 3 2 1

Library of Congress Cataloging-in-Publication Data
Favorite poems of childhood/illustrated by Walter Crane.
p.   cm.
Summary: Well-known nursery rhymes are accompanied by the works of
one of the earliest illustrators of children's books.
1. Nursery rhymes.   2. Children's poetry.   [1. Nursery rhymes.]
I. Crane, Walter, 1845–1915, ill.
PZ8.3.F2364   1993
398.8--dc20   92–42770
CIP
ISBN 0–671–86614–1

The text and pictures of FAVORITE POEMS OF CHILDHOOD have been
selected from THE BABY'S OPERA (1877) and THE BABY'S BOUQUET (1879).
The illustrations have been reproduced from first editions, engraved and
printed by Edmund Evans.

CONTENTS

CONTENTS

Girls and boys come out to play,
The moon it shines as bright as day.
Leave your supper, and leave your sleep,
And join your playfellows in the street.

Come with a whoop, and come with a call,
Come with a good will or not at all.
Up the ladder and down the wall,
A penny loaf will serve you all.

Here we go round the mulberry bush,
The mulberry bush, the mulberry bush.
Here we go round the mulberry bush,
All on a frosty morning.

This is the way we clap our hands,
Clap our hands, clap our hands.
This is the way we clap our hands,
All on a frosty morning.

ORANGES & LEMONS

1 "Oranges and lemons,"
Say the bells of St. Clement's.

2 "You owe me five farthings,"
Say the bells of St. Martin's.

3 "When will you pay me?"
Say the bells of Old Bailey.

4 "When I grow rich,"
Say the bells of Shoreditch.

5 "When will that be?"
Say the bells of Stepney.

6 "I do not know,"
Says the great bell of Bow.

7 Here comes a candle to light you to bed,
And here comes a chopper to chop off your head.

·LAVENDER'S · BLVE ·

Lavender's blue, diddle, diddle!
Lavender's green;
When I am king, diddle, diddle!
You shall be queen.

Call up your men, diddle, diddle!
Set them to work;
Some to the plough, diddle, diddle!
Some to the cart.

Some to make hay, diddle, diddle!
Some to cut corn;
While you and I, diddle, diddle!
Keep ourselves warm.

15

Old King Cole
Was a merry old soul,
And a merry old soul was he.
He called for his pipe,
And he called for his bowl,
And he called for his fiddlers three.

Every fiddler had a fiddle,
And a very fine fiddle had he.
''Tweedle dee, tweedle dee, tweedle dee''
Went the fiddlers three.
O, there's none so rare
As can compare
With King Cole and his fiddlers three.

·KING·COLE·

POLLY
PUT·THE
KETTLE
ON

Polly put the kettle on,
Polly put the kettle on,
Polly put the kettle on,
> *We'll all have tea.*

Sukey take it off again,
Sukey take it off again,
Sukey take it off again,
> *They've all gone away.*

18

·WARM·HANDS·

Warm hands, warm hands,
The men are gone to plough.

If you want to warm your hands,
Warm your hands now.

I saw three ships come sailing by,
 Come sailing by, come sailing by.
I saw three ships come sailing by,
 On New Year's Day in the morning.

And what do you think was in them then,
 Was in them then, was in them then?
And what do you think was in them then,
 On New Year's Day in the morning?

Three pretty girls were in them then,
 Were in them then, were in them then.
Three pretty girls were in them then,
 On New Year's Day in the morning.

And one could whistle, and one could sing,
 The other play on the violin;
Such joy there was at my wedding,
 On New Year's Day in the morning.

·DING·DONG·BELL

Ding dong bell!
Pussy's in the well!
Who put her in?
Little Tommy Lin.
Who pulled her out?
Little Tommy Stout.
What a naughty boy was that,
To try to drown poor pussy cat,
Who never did him any harm,
And killed all the mice in his father's barn.

· PUSS · AT · COURT ·

"*Pussy cat, pussy cat, where have you been?*"
"*I've been up to London to look at the queen.*"
"*Pussy cat, pussy cat, what did you there?*"
"*I caught a little mouse under a chair.*"

Three blind mice,
  See how they run!
They all ran after the farmer's wife,
Who cut off their tails with a carving knife.
Did ever you hear such a thing in your life?
  Three blind mice.

Hickory, dickory, dock!
The mouse ran up the clock.
The clock struck one,
The mouse ran down,
Hickory, dickory, dock!

I HAD A LITTLE NUT TREE

I had a little nut tree,
    Nothing would it bear,
But a silver nutmeg
    And a golden pear.

The King of Spain's daughter
    Came to visit me,
And all for the sake
    Of my little nut tree.

I·HAD·A
LITTLE

N·V·T·
·TREE·

Ye FROG & Ye CROW

1 A jolly fat frog lived in the river swim, O!
A comely black crow lived on the river brim, O!
*   "Come on shore, come on shore,"*
*   Said the crow to the frog and then, O!*
*   "No, you'll bite me, no, you'll bite me,"*
*   Said the frog to the crow again, O!*

2 "O! There is sweet music on yonder green hill, O!
And you shall be a dancer, a dancer in yellow,
*   All in yellow, all in yellow,"*
*   Said the crow to the frog and then, O!*
*   "All in yellow, all in yellow,"*
*   Said the frog to the crow again, O!*

28

3 "Farewell, you little fishes, that in the river
     swim, O!
I'm going to be a dancer, a dancer in yellow."
    "O, beware! O, beware!"
    Said the fish to the frog and then, O!
    "I'll take care, I'll take care,"
    Said the frog to the fish again, O!

4 Then the frog began a-swimming, a-swimming
    to land, O!
And the crow began a-jumping up to give him his
    hand, O!
    "Sir, you're welcome, Sir, you're welcome,"
    Said the crow to the frog and then, O!
    "Sir, I thank you, Sir, I thank you,"
    Said the frog to the crow again, O!

5 "But where is the sweet music on yonder green
    hill, O?
And where are the dancers, the dancers in
    yellow,
    All in yellow, all in yellow?"
    Said the frog to the crow and then, O!
    "Sir, they're here, Sir, they're here,"
    Said the crow to the frog—*

*Here the crow swallows the frog

29

JACK AND JILL

Jack and Jill
Went up the hill,
To fetch a pail of water.
Jack fell down,
And broke his crown,
And Jill came tumbling after.

Up Jack got,
And home did trot,
As fast as he could caper;
Went to bed
To mend his head
With vinegar and brown paper.

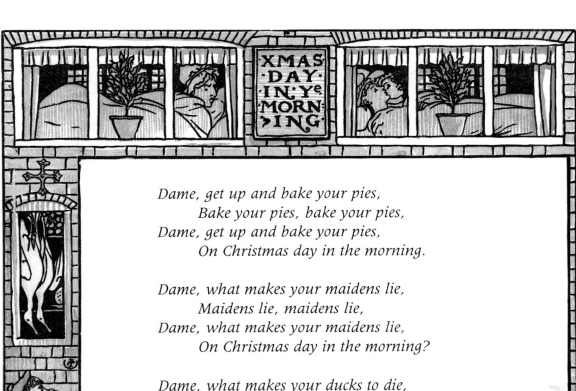

Dame, get up and bake your pies,
    Bake your pies, bake your pies,
Dame, get up and bake your pies,
    On Christmas day in the morning.

Dame, what makes your maidens lie,
    Maidens lie, maidens lie,
Dame, what makes your maidens lie,
    On Christmas day in the morning?

Dame, what makes your ducks to die,
    Ducks to die, ducks to die,
Dame, what makes your ducks to die,
    On Christmas day in the morning?

Their wings are cut, they cannot fly,
    Cannot fly, cannot fly,
Their wings are cut, they cannot fly,
    On Christmas day in the morning.

·LITTLE·JACK·HORNER·

Little Jack Horner
Sat in a corner,
Eating a Christmas pie.

He put in his thumb,
And pulled out a plum,
And said, ''What a good boy am I!''

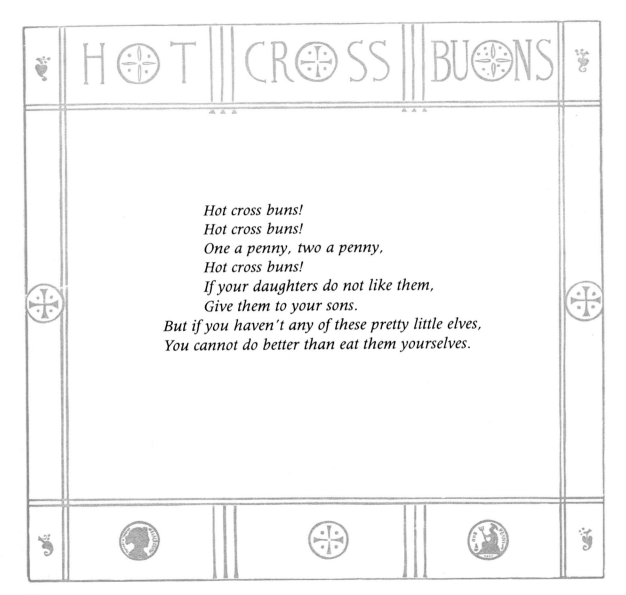

HOT CROSS BUONS

Hot cross buns!
Hot cross buns!
One a penny, two a penny,
Hot cross buns!
If your daughters do not like them,
Give them to your sons.
But if you haven't any of these pretty little elves,
You cannot do better than eat them yourselves.

Ye JOLLY MILLER

There was a jolly miller once
Lived on the river Dee;
He worked and sang from morn to night,
No lark more blithe than he.

And this the burden of his song
Forever used to be,
''I care for nobody, no, not I,
And nobody cares for me.''

A ship, a ship a-sailing,
A-sailing on the sea,
And it was deeply laden,
With pretty things for me.
There were raisins in the cabin,
And almonds in the hold.
The sails were made of satin,
And the mast it was of gold.

The four-and-twenty sailors
That stood between the decks
Were four-and-twenty white mice
With rings about their necks.
The captain was a duck, a duck,
With a jacket on his back,
And when this fairy ship set sail,
The captain he said, ''Quack!''

Little Bo-Peep, she lost her sheep,
    And didn't know where to find them.
Let them alone, they'll all come home,
    And bring their tails behind them.

Little Bo-Peep fell fast asleep,
    And dreamed she heard them bleating.
But when she awoke, she found it a joke,
    For they were still a-fleeting.

Then up she took her little crook,
    Determined for to find them.
She found them indeed, but it made her heart bleed,
    For they'd left their tails behind them.

It happened one day as Bo-Peep did stray
    Into a meadow hard by.
There she espied their tails side by side,
    All hung on a tree to dry.

She heaved a sigh and wiped her eye,
    Then went over hill and dale,
And tried what she could, as a shepherdess would,
    To tack to each sheep its tail.

COCK ROBIN AND JENNY WREN

1 'Twas on a merry time,
        When Jenny Wren was young,
    So neatly as she danced,
        And so sweetly as she sung,
    Robin Redbreast lost his heart.
        He was a gallant bird,
    He doffed his cap to Jenny Wren,
        Requesting to be heard.

2 "My dearest Jenny Wren,
        If you will but be mine,
    You shall dine on cherry pie,
        And drink nice currant wine.
    I'll dress you like a goldfinch,
        Or like a peacock gay,
    So if you'll have me, Jenny, dear,
        Let us appoint the day.

3 Jenny blushed behind her fan
        And thus declared her mind:
    "So let it be tomorrow, Rob,
        I'll take your offer kind.
    Cherry pie is very good,
        And so is currant wine,
    But I will wear my plain brown gown,
        And never dress too fine."

4 Robin Redbreast got up early,
        All at the break of day,
    He flew to Jenny Wren's house,
        And sang a roundelay.
    He sang of Robin Redbreast,
        And pretty Jenny Wren,
    And when he came unto the end,
        He then began again.

40

·HVSH·A·BY BABY·

Hush-a-by, baby, on the tree top,
When the wind blows
The cradle will rock;
When the bough breaks,
The cradle will fall,
And down will come baby, cradle and all!

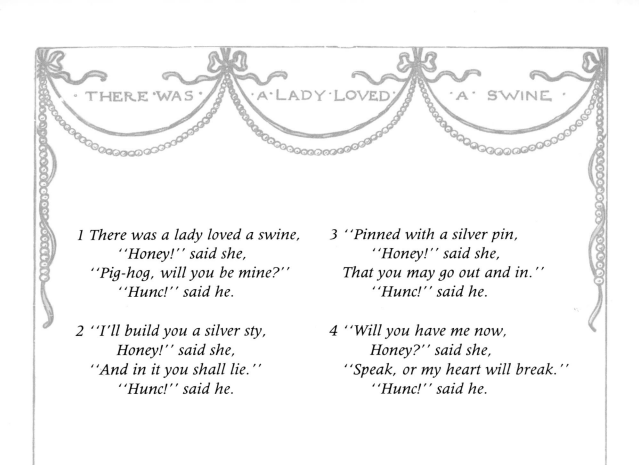

1 There was a lady loved a swine,
      ''Honey!'' said she,
''Pig-hog, will you be mine?''
      ''Hunc!'' said he.

2 ''I'll build you a silver sty,
      Honey!'' said she,
''And in it you shall lie.''
      ''Hunc!'' said he.

3 ''Pinned with a silver pin,
      ''Honey!'' said she,
That you may go out and in.''
      ''Hunc!'' said he.

4 ''Will you have me now,
      Honey?'' said she,
''Speak, or my heart will break.''
      ''Hunc!'' said he.

THERE WAS A LADY LOVED A SWINE

Tom he was a piper's son,
He learned to play when he was young—
But the only tune that he could play
Was ''Over the hills and far away.''
     Over the hills and a long way off,
     The wind shall blow my top-knot off.

Tom with his pipe made such a noise
That he pleased both girls and boys,
And they stopped to hear him play,
''Over the hills and far away.''
     Over the hills and a long way off,
     The wind shall blow my top-knot off.

44